The Circle Dancers

THE CIRCLE DANCERS

Diana Der-Hovanessian

THE SHEEP MEADOW PRESS
RIVERDALE-ON-HUDSON, NEW YORK

All inquiries and permission requests should be addressed to:
The Sheep Meadow Press
P.O. Box 1345
Riverdale-on-Hudson, NY 10471

Designed and typeset by The Sheep Meadow Press.

Printed on acid-free paper in the United States. This book meets the
guidelines for permanence and durability of the Committee on Production
Guidelines for Book Longevity of the Council on Library Resources.

Library of Congress Cataloging-in-Publication Data:

Der-Hovanessian, Diana
     The circle dancers / Diana Der-Hovanessian
          p.   cm.
      ISBN 1-878818-55-4 (alk. paper)
      1. Armenian Americans--Poetry.   I. Title
    PS3554 . E67C57   1996
    811'. 54--dc20   96-30893
                                                   CIP

ACKNOWLEDGMENTS

Grateful acknowledgment is made to the editors of the following publications where many of these poems first appeared: *Agni, American Scholar, Abiko, Ararat, Christian Science Monitor, Die Young, Fork Roads, Graham House Review, Ladies Home Journal, Literary Review, Lyric, Muddy River Review, Negative Capability, Nimrod, Outreach, Poet Lore, Raft, Thirteenth Moon, Yankee.*

CONTENTS

THE PROVERB AS WARNING

REEL

APPLES FROM CHERNOBYL

*For my sister and brother Helen Pahigian
and John Der-Hovanessian Jr.
and for Vahram and Armine*

CIRCLE DANCERS

TEACHING A CHILD TO DANCE

Move with the music but
as if through water
with knees bent imperceptibly,
just barely, for grace.

Move your arms in joy
and let your fingers float,
following wrists as if through
waters that flow.

Let your hand trace a moonrise;
let your fingers harvest grapes
while we glide forward
walking like queens.

Bend slightly, move sprightly
with a springing step
in rhythms of the heart beat
with Anahid and Naneh
guiding your feet.

Move your hands
through the waters of Arax,
palms down, then palms up.
Move with small glides,
magnificent child,
gift of waters and light.

And if you wave a kerchief
wave it leaning back smiling
as if greeting hello and good-bye.

Look over your left shoulder
I am beside you.

And over my left shoulder
my grandmother and hers.
They walk like shy Christian
brides but behind them marching
their pagan mothers
parading with shields.

Look toward your right shoulder
and into your future where
a mother-in-law smiles beckoning
you into a life to be.
The Armenian dance is a dance of women,
friends in a circle that opens
and closes and never ends.

CIRCLE DANCE

Bar, *the Armenian word for dance*
comes from the Dacian word for circle.
— John Greppin, linguist

The Dacian word for circle
comes from the Armenian word for dance.
— Lillian Murad, dance historian

In my dream I am nineteen again
in a circle at the old Twenty-
Third Street Y.

My red hair is streaked
from the sun, although
there is no sun in the studio.

Lillian Murad has come, legendary
Lillian who dances like a doe
and spins stories about the pagan

past of each step.
The circle is the dance of life
she says, showing how it opens, closes.

Suddenly in my dream
I am in the center
asking, "Is this how?"

Nevart joins me and we mirror
each other's arm movements.
I want to tell her how

glad I am to see her again
when Arsen and Eddie leap in.
"Eddie! I thought you died

in that horrible cleaning-plant fire."
He stares furiously out of
yellowed coal eyes and hisses,

"How could I die? How could I do that
to my parents after they survived a genocide
to get me born in New Jersey?"

"Forgive me," I say while Lillian nods:
"You are doing the Naz Bar perfectly.
Do you know the Dacian word for circle?"

THE KOCHARI

This is the village dance
done by the old men
who rise slowly to shuffle
one behind the next.
Forward and backward
the dancers bounce
in a reel that gets livelier
quickening each step.

The dancers grow younger,
younger as they move
like climbers climbing
toward their youth,
shuffling off years until
the younger men join in.

Once reserved for males
this country dance
of slide-step and stamping
is joined by women now,
not so much in defiance
as savoring what rebounds.

MAY I HAVE THIS DANCE?

May I have this dance? Father would bow.
One of us would leap on Father's feet,
hanging on to his hands as if we knew how,

riding his shoes as if on the prow
of a huge ship journeying into the deep
rhythms of dancing. Father would bow

thanking one partner and then allow
another to leap on his toes to sweep
into a waltz as if knowing how.

We'd follow the steps of polka or loud
march. Whatever the tune it was always sweet
and brief until Father would bow

toward Mother laughing (I hear her now).
They never danced; it was our treat.
We didn't realize he didn't know how.

His childhood was stolen, but he endowed
ours with laughter as we rode his feet
lifting us over the past somehow.
Father would thank us and solemnly bow.

LAUGHTER

Like a campfire that draws
a magic ring around its fold,
it can leave those outside
its circle in the cold.

AT TWILIGHT

The two syllables of their names
ripple over the yard to pass
unheard. "Maro, Sona, come home."

It is twilight and the color's drained
from pink dogwood and the tall grass.
The syllables of the two names

do not interrupt their games,
old games with a cast of ghosts.
"Maro, Sona, children, come home."

Not that games stay the same,
not that anything can last,
only the syllables of their names

which no one answers to, or claims.
Children turn invisible at dusk.
Maro and Sona do not come home.

Children at twilight blend with the rain.
But against the coming night their names
form the syllables that bless
the dark: "Maro, Sona, come home."

HOW TO GROW A SAILOR

Start with a mother
who never shows
her fear of water.
Start with a father
with respect for
the unknown.

Let the children be held
around the waist
as they float on placid
water. Let them shout:
Let go. Let go,
full of trust
of liquid light.

Let them grow up
in love with depth
and mystery. Let them
float over nights
raked by a metallic moon.

Let them go to sleep
hearing old stories
of islands reached
only by full blown sails.

WATCHING CHILDREN DANCE

"How can we know the dancer from the dance?"
I ask, quoting Yeats. And you say
as we admire the children's exuberance,

"Do you have problems with lancer and his lance?
And what about the player and his play?
Can you tell the glancer from his glance?

And what about the panter and his pants,
doer with deed, weigher and his weigh.
Watch the children swaying in exuberance.

Their laughter blends music and jubilance;
you see the difference between laugh and sway.
Why not in the dancer and the dance?

Their teachers instructing them to advance
and retreat as if rehearsing a ballet
do not confuse the stander and the stance,

poet and poems, romancer and romance.
They see the line between sun and ray."
But those who truly dance with exuberance
feel no difference in dancer and dance.

SEAGULLS

There must have been birds, the first
which circled shrieking, that fall day
their shrill warnings that burst
welcoming through the mist and spray.
There must have been gulls which dived
at those three Spanish sailing boats,
birds to announce they had arrived
at land which might at any moment float
toward them. The sailors must have sighed
the Spanish words for gull and sky
pointing at wings riding the tide
lithe scavengers with beady eye
      harbingers of rest and port
      turning their labor into sport.

RUNNING

Not marathons,
although that kind has
its own exhilaration

and I am not unmindful
of Greek origins
and the identity

of the last winner
in ancient
times, Varasdat
the Armenian,

showing how
strangers can
take trophies after all;

and not the fear
haunted pace along dark
city streets,

nor the dash for the plane,
a rattling heart
loose in the ribs.

No, the kind of running
I mean is seen

from train windows:
small boys rushing by
waving, waving,

or a girl in a distant
field of daisies
her hair aloft

and in your mind's eye
a father waiting
in their car
for her return,
her arms full of
black-eyed flowers.

SONG OF THE CRANE

BREAK IN

Sawdust, a stream of litter on the floor,
the door inside the outside door ajar,
the contents of each dining room drawer
emptied, strewn as if a giant had poured

out everything. I ran screaming to call
911, aghast at the chaos inside
the bedroom, the lingerie a tide
of silk and nylon flowing to the hall.

"Table silver, all jewelry, an old photo
of my father at four in a village dress
the only thing his mother saved, pressed
on the inside of a brooch, an old cameo,

my mother's, my great aunt's rings."
Police ask for listings of such things.

* * *

I gave them the inventory, everything
I remembered: My former husband's war
medals, his silver officer's bars,
my child's first tooth, pearls, my wedding ring.

The detective asked if I'd been robbed before.
I thought of jewels buried in the ground
as Armenian families fled the sound
of shooting, Turks breaking in each door,

my grandmother's gems down to one cameo
sent to America with her older son,
two million relatives lost as one,
art, architecture, poems I'd never know,
everything except a picture in a cameo.
Answered what he wanted, "No."

29

SONG OF THE CRANE

"You mean stork, stork," said Czeslaw Milosz
when I told him I had gone eight thousand
miles to see Armenian cranes.

"No. Storks," he corrected nodding
at my description of the exiles'
bird bringing news from every roof
to the wandering villager far from home.

"But" I said, "Storks bring babies
here in America. They cannot bring
other kinds of news. They must be
translated into graceful cranes."

"Storks" he repeated rolling
the "r" making me laugh but
afraid to ask what bird it was
he asked not to visit him again.
What bird was it in whose disguise
the dead return? Was it the crane?

"Storks" he answered my
unasked question.

TRANSLATING

1. I Was Born Bilingual But...

The Armenian language
is the music of my childhood,
the sweet taste
of everything that was home.
It is my lost treasure,
halved and bartered;
the dream that comes to haunt
my English language dream.
It is the echo of the ages,
the shadow of old giants,
but palpable, yes, we made it.
We are a part of it, this gift
we are letting drift away.

2. Old Words

Sometimes it takes five words
of buoyant, tensile English
to explain one ancient leathery word.

Old words lie weighted, glittering
for centuries in the sun
like brittle stones.

And Armenian words have worn thin
like old coins, changed, exchanged in vain,

gaining a soft patina unmatched
except by old monasteries in the rain.

Their meanings have grown ironic
with a subtle subliminal drone.
Take the word for justice, for instance,
with its satiric overtones.

3. Custom

Words are not lifeless.
They live in houses;
they grow and they are fed.
In Armenia "Dada" is grandmother,
the second hovering figure
over baby's head.

4. Words Are Made of Breath,

larynx, lip and tongue.
Print and paper are silent signs
of what should be sung.

The Arabs say every new language
gives the learner an added soul.

The Irish say Celtic silence
cannot be recast or retold.

The Armenians say their language
is translated only by the heart.

Italians laugh saying music
is the translator's taunt, not art.

NOAH'S RAVENS
(For Hovhanness Shiraz)

He called us Noah's crows,
we of the diaspora, ravens
who have not come home
to roost.

"Does that make you
left in the homeland
doves of peace and love?"
I asked the Armenian poet.

He called us Noah's crows,
laughing of course,
but meaning every word.

"Why don't you come back
where you belong?" he said lying
on his deathbed. (I didn't know
it was his deathbed then.)

"Why don't you return,
dispersed crows, who squawk
in foreign tongues?
Especially you, my swan
standing silent there."

"Isn't it too late?
We have become exiles by profession
at home everywhere,
at home nowhere.

Homesick everywhere
homesick for a place
never seen until middle age,

homesick for a language
we speak only to ourselves."

"While there's life
there's change. Look at me,"
he said, "I am going to America."

"You are going there to live?"

"No. I'm going to America
to speak to Noah's crows.
If you get there first
tell them to come home."

RECYCLING TODAY

So this is the day we get back
at the end of our lives
the day we can have again
to relive twenty four hours?

"Recycling Today" says the banner
across the gate of the University
of Massachusetts, Boston
where I drive north on the Southeast
Expressway past the glittering bay.

Today recycled?
Not a bad one
with its intense sun.
I smile at drivers passing me
who scowl at my pace, not realizing
they frown on recycle day.

"What day will you have back again"
Antranig Zarougian wrote,
"on your dying day,
if it were given, if it were given
to relive again?"

"Not my wedding day,"
he answered himself. "Not the day
of the birth of my child.
Not the hour of my greatest success.
But one day from my lost
childhood. Any day."

Any one day,
when there was such a thing
as childhood.

Before the genocide.

Before the nation
was orphaned. Any day
before we know we are cut down.

And this is the day,
driving, rolling along
not cut down, smiling in the sun.
The day we'll have back.

"Don't choose a special day"
Thornton Wilder advised.
"An ordinary day
will be extraordinary enough."

I will telephone everyone
to tell them the good news.
When all else is lost
we will have this day.

CHARM AGAINST INERTIA

I fight listlessness
with energy from the steam
rising on the Black Sea.

My grandfather,
Hagop is walking
toward it, through Kharpet
to Samsun,
and the boat for Marseilles
and America.

He is thirteen.
He enters a dark forest
of brush and snakes
to pass water and gets lost.

He runs. He falls,
cuts his leg against
a stump. The scar will last
sixty three years past
1879.

But wait;
he finds the others
and they all reach the port.

The Turkish boatman
paid by their families,
demands another payment
to row them to the ship for America.

What shall we do?

Hagop has a plan: We will pay him

because we must get on the boat.
Trust me.

The oarsman delivers them to the ship.
He holds out the paper
for signatures he needs
to get the rest of his fee.

No, says Hagop, once aboard.
We won't sign.
Unless you give back the money
you cheated us of, on the shore.

It is returned with a shrug.
The mist rises from the water
like gauze, and I watch
the boat sail toward me.

FOUR AND FIVE

Four and five years old—
we are on the other side
of the highway from our house
and I see the boy in a green
snowsuit. (What is he doing
there in April?) (In later memories
there is no boy, no snowsuit
no visitors of any kind)
but he is there and we rush
across the street.
Tell it how it was.
I rush. I rushed.
I rush. I do not look.
I looked. There were no cars.
We cross. But never reach
the other side. Each night
for all my childhood I try
to cross and never reach.
I fall and try to crawl
and try to find my sister
whom I led across the road
on which the yellow
truck appears
to strike us down
but I get up. She does not move.
And still lies on the road.
I rise, try to wake her too.
I run. Behind me the driver comes
carrying her like a flat doll.
He is still walking
up to my grandmother who screams.
My mother stands silent across
the years.
Mother, forgive me for taking

the comfort of your old age —
father, for cutting
the family portrait
after so many cuts,
for robbing you of a force
that might have changed
the weather of the world.

APRICOT TREES

She calls to tell me they are cutting
the apricot trees in Armenia.

You can't be serious, I gasp.

They are freezing. And there
is no other fuel.

But what about the fruit for next year?
I don't say "blossoms".
I don't say "petaled light".
I don't say "trees like haloed angels".
I don't say "trees like veiled brides".

I say What about next
year's harvest?

She interrupts saying
There is no heat. There might not be
a next year.

She pauses, waits for forgiveness,
for the absolution no one can give.

FROM A LETTER I DID NOT RECEIVE

We are burning books
in Yerevan. For heat.
The poplars that lined
the streets are gone.
The flowering apricot
won't bloom this spring.
The limbs were cut
but did not keep us warm.

You, you who hear
the steam heat rise,
and boil water for tea,
taste everything twice,
please, once for me.

WHAT IF

What if all the poets were rounded up and killed?
What if all the priests were executed?
What if all the men in the country
were drafted and then shot in front of ditches
they themselves had dug?
What if the government said: In two days
you must leave your home and belongings
taking only enough for two days on the road?
What if all the pretty girls were raped?
What if small children were taken
by families who wanted slaves
or pets? What if everyone in your family
was pushed into the Euphrates?
What if you alone, with an older girl,
made it to Baku?
What if in Baku you met compatriots
who had been there for centuries
and there you grew?
What if you lived until old age
with your children and then again
eight years ago men came
and burned your home again?
What if you were forced again to leave?
What if you reached other Armenians
in Karabagh?
What if they were being bombed and maimed
and blockaded?
What if you were asked again to leave?
What if you were over eighty
and everything that had happened to you
was happening again
and again the world did not believe you?
What if it were you and not me.

EVERY WOMAN

Every woman who has loved you, every hand
that pressed, caressed, shaped the man
you've become, every female — mother, child
who claimed, tamed, calmed or drove you wild;
every woman in your life I bless,
thanking them for this happiness.

Whether redemption or temptation to your soul,
whether she pulled you apart or made you whole,
everyone you've loved I love from your past,
everywhere you walked, every shadow cast.
But I can't promise to care for (should there be)
a successor. Let her love me.

LOVE POEM

This is a love poem
that changes
the way love changes
and the way poems change
with time and with readers.
This is a love poem for you
who thought we had forgotten you
with our coldness
with our indifference
with our foreign tongues
with our foreign names
far away from you.

This is a love poem
for two million
shadows who walk with us
because they can find
no other hearts to haunt.

This is a love poem
made of silence
for the silent
by the silent.

This is a love poem
by the silent who have finally
decided to speak.

This is a love poem that turns
into a political poem.

This political poem
addresses left and right
and all the rights

a political poem should address,

all the rights of human dignity
which the silent were denied
in life and death

the right to speak
the right to be heard

all the rights they never had

the right to breathe in and breathe out
all the rights they never had

the right to close one's eyes
in a peaceful natural death,

all the rights they never had,
they, who were wrenched from
life with unspeakable tortures.

The political poem accosts
all other poems that avoid
and look away...to say

Now look here.

These shadows are not going
to go away unless light
is shed on them and their cause.

If the Armenian case is forgotten
the shadows cast by 1915
which have already lengthened
lengthened with Hitler, with Stalin,
with Cambodia making the 20th century

the century of shadows.

If light is not finally shed
on their cause
the 20th century stain
will continue to spread until
we are plunged into another dark age,

and its people will forget
how to write a political poem
how to read a political poem,
how to write a love poem
how to feel a love poem
how to feel anything at all.

THE PROVERB AS WARNING

THE PROVERB AS WARNING

Don't walk on hot coals
unless you have consulted your feet.

Save your breath when you
make a request of the deaf.

Don't press hands too tightly
at parting unless you mean hello.

Before you devote your life to song
find out who wants to hear you sing.

No one can live up to
the fantasies created by
long distance courtship.

Silent love sounds
the same as indifference.

CHICKEN RIDDLE

Why does the chicken cross the road?
That was no chicken; that was my wife.

How did your wife cross your path?
That was no road, that was my life.

Why did you follow her through the rye?
She was someone else then; so was I.

Why did you chicken out of the game?
Before I looked at spring, my winter came.

MUSE

Tonight, feverish, head-aching, trying to sleep
I mumbled "Leave me alone", then leaped
up, frightened you might really go,

to write the words you dictated one by one,
wondering who (you or me) was meant
as the lost exile you wanted found.

I could sleep without you prodding me awake;
and read merely for pleasure's sake.
Without you my day's pace, quick or slow

would be guiltless. I could lie in the sun
or work without your persistent
"It didn't happen unless it's written down."

FOR STANLEY KUNITZ READING

The poems he reads
solidify into
objects we can hold

like his pears
yellow and cold
each with a green leaf flag.

Each poem unfolds,
redeems, another
anguished memory.

The old portrait
his mother ripped
becomes whole.

A LITTLE SALT

Oh, said the anthropology
professor, looking at my name,
I *thought* you were one
of the "big-eyed people".

Yes, I have the look
of those people grown
wide-eyed staring at horizons
for justice to arrive,

with Armenian eyes,
slightly down turned
from disappointment.

"And you know," he continued
"Russians call you
the salted ones because
a bit of salt is added
to your baptismal water."

A little salt
as souvenir of seas
we came from, seas we lost,

a bit of salt
for sweat and
hospitality's table,

a little bit of salt
for brightening
the tarnished,

a little salt
for preservation

of Christ's mass,

a bit of salt
so the "big eyed"
will bathe in tears
for once and all,
needing no more.

JOHN BERRYMAN PLAYING CHESS
(For Benjamin Houston Brown)

John Berryman in Paris
playing chess
admitted what he loved
the best was death.
At fifteen
outside his window
he found a suicide,
his father. And decided
then it would be up
to him to choose when.
He would control death
if not life. He let
others manage time —
a wife (or two or four).
Others arranged his days;
he showed up on time
if in a whisky haze.
His dissertation was
on Stephen Crane. Over chess
he admitted it was
with Hart he was obsessed.
Hart's leap from
the boat bridge. Berryman,
we shouted, finish
the Dream Songs you began.
For God's sake. Death
is not a game to lose.
When he leaped it was
not unexpected news.
He had been sold.
And no one could buy
him back. It was knowing
he struck ice first
that made us cry.

PROMETHEA
or What Prometheus's Wife Said

Unlike the feminine moon
who borrows light

I was the one who
got fire to ignite.

I discovered warmth;
I discovered flame.

While you screamed: Watch out,
you'll burn down the cave!

Then shouting your name
you went on parade

ran with my torch to brag
"Look at what I made!"

GOYA

The painter of blank eyes
drained dry of tears,
of bulging bellies
and thick royal furs,

rapacious invaders,
their starving prey,
children without childhood,
the hanged, the flayed,

painted a milkmaid
just before his death,
in silken skin, in pink
radiant health.

UNINVITED

She didn't believe in paradise
and so it was a shock
to see its shining towers rise and
find them barred and locked.

LOSING THE UPPER HAND

Unspoken love may be
hunger and thirst

but it's a big risk for
the one who speaks first.

TRAVEL OPENS THE EYES

The Taj was what I went to see
by moonlight. It took years and all
my savings. Now I can't recall
my going there as actuality.
But beetles, spice and sweat,
the thin cows looming like ghosts
along the airport road still float
into my dreams. Sleepers in streets.

Back home again the marble lace
and reflecting pool fade
back into photographs. What stays
with me is the street person's face.
Here it is again, — beard, flies,
in Cambridge. This time I meet his eyes.

THE SILVERFISH

What you don't know won't
hurt you but can make you
twitch in your sleep, trying
to switch it off your eye
lid where it (lightly) creeps
to the floor where it owns
all of the dark. And if you've
never found it parked
inside your morning cup,
its thousand feet up —
thrust and dried, your sleep will
be much sounder through the night.

THE GRAY VILLANELLE

We did not meet when our hair was gold or brown.
Still, you're the handsomest man I've known.
We did not share a past in any town.

It's too late now to change time that's gone
or shift life's patterns. We might <u>not</u> have grown
closer when your hair was gold, or brown.

I do not know if we are fortune's pawn
nor what molded you so that you've become
the handsomest man I've ever known.

I cannot share in the time that's flown.
We cannot see beyond the present, pale and wan.
We did not meet when we were gold or brown.

Too many count on us to stay theirs alone.
Too late to be itinerant. But let me own
you are the handsomest of all I've known.

And so we merely bow and are gone
advising others "Carpe diem, all's on loan".
We did not meet when our hair was gold or brown
when it could have altered all we've known.

IN 1979

While arranging a poetry reading
at Boston University for a Russian poet
I was assigned help from Elena
from alumni administration.

My first book had come out.

"Do you know how good you are?"

"Well," I said, "I would have stayed
in advertising if I thought I were bad."

"It's the same thing" said Elena.
"Poems advertise the poet."

"No" I objected. "That's not the point.
The reader has to find himself in..."

"It's all show biz. And I could do a lot
for you if you'd let me.
You dress all wrong for a poet."

I looked down at my little tweed
skirt, my loafers. 1979.

"You should wear long peasant skirts,
heavy jewelry. And a cape. Always a cape."

I laughed.

"You laugh too much." she said. "People
don't take you seriously. You have to
wear a black cape and arrive late.
You're always early. Make people

wait. Have heads turn."

"But that wouldn't be me."

"Of course it would. Your poems say
'Hey, look at me.' Why can't your clothes?"

"My poems say, I hope this speaks
to you."

"No. Poems say, Look at this cape."

SONG

If you loved me, he said,
you would learn my own tongue
and translate poems
I wanted sung.

I did and I did
until I ran out of ink
and tears from my hollow eyes
filled the kitchen sink.

If you loved me, he said,
you would wear black net
open toe shoes
and never get wet.

I did and I did
until I lost friends and foes
from Harper's and Vogue
and got pigeon toes.

If you loved me, he said
you'd cook vegetarian meals
and drink only milk
from aphids and eels.

And I did and I did
until I saw him one noon
eating the fatted calf
at the Chocolate Spoon.

If you loved me you'd let me
go now, he said.
And I did. But first shot him
twice through the head.

REEL

NO MAESTRO
(Composition without title
or conductor by John Cage)

If you feel a need
for a name
an address
a nationality
an era
a past
history
a people
to belong to
in time

you will forget
that need in
music
that has no
conductor.
Each line belongs
only to itself;
each note knows
where it leads.
It does not mind
falling by chance
on deaf ears.
No one accounts;
no one describes it.
No one has built
a floor plan
or sketched
a staircase to climb.
No one is in charge.

Someone made it, yes.
Some one plays it,
perhaps.
And if you hear it
you might name it.
The composer allows
that much.

ONE MORE

"How many poems can you write about New York City at night?"
Charles Simic

Maybe one more
about drifting news
papers, about
being fearful of every
approaching shadow,
about shadows with
the depth of Joseph
Cornell collages,
about passing people
afraid of you.
Maybe one more about
lights reminding you
of architecture's reach.
One more saying "Tonight
a corned beef sandwich,
tomorrow, the world."

CIRCLING

Once in winter from the window
of a bus going to Providence
I saw a pair of white swans
swimming in a small pond
surrounded by snow everywhere.
Slowly they were circling,
circling without pause
in the cold air. And I
came home to write letters
you would not get, but which
kept the ice from forming.

BATHING THE BABY
IN TIME OF DROUGHT

Later the video will show her
drinking the bath water
as it is poured

over her, opening her mouth
to the liquid warmth,
laughing.

Outside is a dry season
of heat; inside, cool
camera light.

She laughs, and we forget
the drought and her
ancestors walking

beside wagons
through blazing air
toward the Great Salt Lake.

We forget the other
relatives marching
through the parched desert

to Syria and beyond.
She laughs at water
and we laugh.

THE MOMENT THAT STAYS

is that one beside the mountain stream
so clear we can see the trout
hiding in the grassy current
while we try coaxing a small child out

from where he has waded barefoot
to walk his slippery hold,
laughing when we insist he'll freeze
because we are so cold.

REEL

Handing clothes to her
from the basket of wet laundry
we had carried out together
with our uneven height and gait
I look up as she shakes
each piece and pins it overlapping
with the next. Sunshine gilds
the grass. A breeze lifts her red
brown hair, then fills the sheets
like sails to whirl around the reel.
We laugh as they twirl, white, white
from the bluing rinse, white
as her hair is now while I fold
warm sheets from the dryer for her bed.

WINTER IN WYOMING

In November the roads close
and the mountains and
black hills, "Paha Sepa"
"black with pine" turn pale.

The Lakota Sioux country
of spruce and aspen
belongs again to antelope,
sleeping bear and elk.

Plumes of mist at Medicine Bow
rise like eagles over
the evergreen, like smoke
from Indians long decamped

while you lie in a warm bed
in a silver spangled dream
of white mountains
white rabbits and white doe.

INVISIBLE

At the Flying Horses of the small
carnival near the reservation,
Riverton, Wyoming, where we stop
for ice cream, little Arapaho
children like unblinking dolls
in silver studded denim, descend
from the carousel each holding
a grown up's hand. I try
catching a father's eye to smile
in gratitude for the wide skied
wild flowered land we have been
driving through. But no gaze meets
mine. I have never arrived.

SOMETHING ABOUT CONNECTIONS

Maro and I stoop to uncoil
strings of Christmas lights,
loops of green, spangled with
tiny bulbs piled up in a box,
green wire that will disappear
between small stars it unites.
Each light will be separate,
unconnected, crystal bright,
shining like remembered days
beyond ordinary time.
Maro hands me sparkling strings,
while I make a silent wish, —
about invisible connections,
about this child, this night.

FIRST SNOW, LAST SNOW

White, — pieces of light,
luminescent, light filled white,
thin sliced opal, or mica diced,
chalk dust, rock dust, flakes of ice,
silken, milky, petals of peach,
melting even as we reach.

IS LOVE ENDLESS?

Well, he said, for years,
for centuries, we have believed
in the eternal, the resurrected,
the reincarnate, and the kingdom come,
that comes without going.
The everlasting, while all the while
the rain washes it away
with the snowman that guarded
the snowfort.
If spring goes, spring returns;
if love goes, it takes its home
with it. And there is nothing, no
where to return.

You have forgotten, she said,
your mother. And the fierce cling
of roots. The harder you pull
the hardier they grow. You have
forgotten the insistence of habit
and the inclination of genes.
You have forgotten the endless
stretch of stars and the infinity
in the microscope.

On the other hand, he said:
the throw away society
has begun its roll call.
But on this hand, she reminded him
energy cannot be consumed.

HOUSES OF AMSTERDAM

Like the houses
of Amsterdam
looking firmly shored
but ready to float
out all their household
goods and gods
on moving boats
every first of May,
I am ready,
if not to float,
to let you float.
Exits are easy.
Walk down the stone steps
to the barge. Look.
Central bearing beams jut
out of every house,
unexpected perches
for gulls, but built
to hoist all
furniture. Like these
houses we come equipped —
even if not willing.

ON THE LONGEST DAY OF THE YEAR

At noon in Alexandria
more than two thousand years ago
Eratosthenes stared
at the shape of a shadow

made by the stick which
he had planted in the ground
to help him deduce the earth
was not flat but round.

He found the earth's circumference
curving like a ball
without imagining how far
his own shadow would fall.

BLACKBERRY SUMMER

Betty Carlson and I
were both five that summer,
but born to different eras.

She was an only child brought
up thinking she was adult.

I was protected from all knowledge
of evil before the burden of
an Armenian past became mine.

The summer we were five,
we would wander through West
Auburn woods picking blackberries,
raspberries, blueberries
that stained the sunlight
and jeweled our tongues.

That was the year we saw the tramp
along the railroad tracks.

She knew what to do.
I would have kept walking
and said hello.
I would have shown him
the loaded blueberry bushes
if he looked hungry.

She pushed me into low shrubs
and put her hand over my mouth
choking down my giggles,
as the man went by us,
close enough to touch.

He passed by and
down the tracks
singing until he disappeared,
singing as if he were alone,
imagining his walk
would end at dusk and not
go on forever in my mind.

"Why did we hide?"

"Because he could have killed us."

I laughed out loud.
No. There are no Turks here
to do that.
For, in spite of all my parent's
care, I had heard the whispers.

OTHER

What does that word mean,
the one that sounds like "odor"?

— "Odahr"? It means
"other" or non-Armenian.

You mean everyone who is not Armenian
is called an "odahr" by Armenians?

— That's not so bad. In Greece
anyone not Greek is called "barbaros".

Barbarian? At one time they were right.
Someone told me "odahr" means alien.

— Yes, foreigner, with no implications.
It means simply non-Hai.

Oh, come now. No implications?

— Simply not Hai.

You call yourselves Hai. That comes
from the Hittite?

— Probably. I was married to a non Hai.

You were married to an "odahr"?

— Well, he looked Armenian.

Does that mean he had sad brown eyes? You don't.

— At an Armenian gathering some years ago

someone asked him if his wife were Armenian.

You?

— Sure, he answered, I wouldn't marry an "odahr"

QUILT

It was pieced
swatch by swatch
from premiums of old time
cigarette packs,

pictures of American
presidents
matched
with squares of velvets

that I leaned against,
a checkerboard
of famous men
Grandmother patched

to cover new guests,
refugees from peril
and pain,
with an American past.

THE POET MAGICIAN
(for Gerald Stern)

Do not enter his poem.
There is no way that
you will get out,
except through dark
and twisting hallways with
no light switch to turn on.

If you grope long enough
a wall will fall and you
will be out in a gray winter
on the West Side of New York

with the 1941 Red Army
hunched into greatcoats
at the end of each street.
Leningrad burns in their
eyes. And no switch
can turn off the blaze.

Do not enter this poem.
While you look for a way
to escape
                    vandals with
baseball bats will smash
your car parked outside.

Do not enter his poem.
It is 1946 and cold.
Rikers and the White Tower
open their doors in steamy
splendor, peopled
with all of your past.

You will find you never
left anyone anywhere,
never escaped from a thing.
His poem finds it
and drags it back.

COMING UP FOR AIR

I who never learned
to swim right
walk through this water
with you, with tanks,
new lungs, on our backs,
new eyes that show me
creatures who do not fear
us any more than
other fish.
You float above me and
there is no such thing
as fire to feed or tamp.
My former life is swallowed
by deaf tides.
The songs are all new
and wordless. I open
my hand as if it were a fin.

APPLES FROM CHERNOBYL

STATUES OF HAIG

The statues of Yerevan
in illustrated books
flex bronze muscles
that photograph bright black.

Flicking pages
I remember tales
from Radio Yerevan
that claimed

the Kremlin ordered
statues commissioned
after Stalin's death
to have heads that screwed
off and on.

Yerevan's statues in books
are mostly heads,
bronze busts
with literary smiles,

or mounted legends,
David of Sassoun,
flying on his horse
both East and West,

or Haig Nahabet
father of us all,
leaning back
for that one arrow
meant for Pel;

thighs like trunks of trees,
stories rooted

in an ancient place,
heroes measured by wars,
myths taking the male form.
Silk on stone.

I think of you,
and turn the page,
remembering metaphors
I was too shy to say.
Those legs, yes, and
Haig's arrow
I was spared,
Armenian legends
that I bless
and others can embrace.

APPLES

Three apples fell from heaven,
one from Eve, one from Atalanta,
and one from Lethe's shore.

One was the fruit of knowledge,
one, the fruit of love,
one of forgetting.

Ah, now there is a fourth,
said the Russian poet,
the fruit of revenge.

There are stories making
the rounds after the Chernobyl
nuclear tragedy

how tainted crops supposedly
destroyed were smuggled
into markets or shipped

to other areas for sale.
Apples from Chernobyl,
Apples from Chernobyl,

the old woman vendor calls.
What are you doing, Babushka?
Are those really contaminated?

No. But you'd be surprised
how well they sell.

How well they sell?
Apples you call poisoned?

Yes, yes,
apples for stepmothers,
apples for your rival,
apples for your boss,

Apples for plagiarists,
apples for slanderers,
apples for villains everywhere.

Weapons for the weaponless,
for victims, for the defenseless,
buy apples here.

Three apples fell from the past,
one from Isis, fruit of unpolluted air,
one from Anahid, the fruit of sacred earth,

and one from Demeter, fruit of history
that time alone can grow.
There was no fourth.

OLINDO

You have become the map
of the lost Armenian provinces.
I wake with the syllables
of your rivers on my lips.
Your eyes look east;
their blue has turned to gray
smoke, your hands to leaves
bronzed in the sun of Yerevan.
Your eyes, calmed, do not smolder
anymore. They are the skies
reflected in the steel of Sevan.
Your hands are winds
of Manti on a cloudless day.

The first words you spoke to me
were in Italian. Dante.
I never found the lines
but they echo in my dreams.
Your voice speaks in Armenian now,
your face is the sun
on yellow tufa temples,
the sun of Haghartsin warming
convents filled with ghosts.

Your hands that I clasped
in friendship hold me up.
Your arms encircling me
once to say good-bye float away
with your golden body
on the Mediterranean.
Your whisper reaches
the Caspian shores.
I have forgotten your voice.
Your lips that kissed me

just once and made me laugh
kissing an ink spot
on my face, that kiss
has turned into a hundred poems.

LILAC SUNDAY

Let us agree to meet
here some winter
when the park

gates are locked,
and the arches thinned
of their vaulting green

to climb the wall,
thaw the icicles
and watch them rain

like flowering
cherry and lilacs
that kissed your hair;

some winter
when the fog is heavy, —
to return to this light.

SOMETHING ABOUT LILACS

Your postcard is illegible. A blot of rain
helps me imagine something about lilacs,
thousands still in bloom

somewhere in the north. Dark stains
of purple against leaves while ours
have showered down in chaff

and dry perfume. Somewhere north.
New Foundland? Moscow? Maine,
where they flower in your words

unreadable as the names
for lilacs in Armenia's Taurus
mountains where the first bushes came

or the forgotten American Indian words
for blossoms that marked settlement
and white man's domain.

AFTER THE EARTHQUAKE

The steam heat rises
the electric blanket snaps on.
Flannel sheets, cozy and warm, pull
you toward sleep. Why do you stay awake
and wait for walls to crack
and ice to swallow every road you have taken?

In Leninakan, in Armenia
there was a rumbling.

And then the huge blasts.
"We thought the Russian subterranean
arms factory had exploded."

"We thought the Azerbaijanis
had set off the underground munition works."

"We knew the Azerbaijanis had bombed
the Russian underground arms."

"It was sabotage, on the fault line."

"It was sabotage not God.
It was man, not weather."

Today's news, headlines,
television pictures
catch the breath of the world until
a fresh catastrophe, a new war,
another city trembles or burns.

On foreign screens the flashing of
destruction, ancient cathedrals
given another blow,

one hundred thousand deaths
of one hundred thousand refugees
who had escaped from Azerbaijan
crushed or lost in pits and cavities
365 villages collapsed,
arable land destroyed,
farm animals killed,
schools and children
homes and factories,
art and artist.

Leninakan's pictures
flashed over the world
but the world's prayers
do not reach Leninakan.

At night a small voice from
the short wave wireless:
"We are a small people.

Our buildings have collapsed.
Our hearts are bleak. Why
has this too been put on our shoulders?"

On December 14th:
"Why is there no answer?
There are many suicides among
the survivors."

December 15th wireless:
"We have to believe that we are not alone."

Yes, you have to believe you are not alone.
We have to believe we are not alone.

We are part of you. You are part of us.

Whatever happens to you happens to us.
If you are lost, we are lost.

If we are lost you lose an echo
a mirror and half your soul.
If we lose you we lose our past,
our soul, our hope and our future.

— — — —

The steam heat rises, the tea kettle boils,
the electric blanket hums, but nothing,
nothing, nothing warms.

MOVSES AND SEVAN

This water, this gently undulating lake,
gray as the eyes of the girl from
your lost childhood, this deep Sevan,
was not always a lake.

It was a dream; it was a mist;
it was a woman in veils. Water
is not always visible.

Sometimes it floats in fog,
falls in snow, hides in unshed tears
or underground rivers
inside the cistern of a stone
heart. Sevan was not always a lake.

It used to shimmer in the wet eyes
of the thirsty peasants who walked
through the wooded hills
and valleys between.

Sevan was the village fountain.
It was a valley of clover, a sea of bees,
a vineyard of green grapes, an orchard
of apricots belonging to the village
with its name.

In those days Sevan was an artesian

trickle of water bubbling
out of the ground, a spring covered
by a huge wooden lid. Long before it was a lake
it watered the valley and the village.

The peasants lifted the lid to fill

jug and jars with
clear spring water that crackled
with flakes of cold light.

An old law, no, a superstition about
the lid, convinced everyone that if
the fountain were left uncapped it would overflow
to drown the valley. Or the spring
would run out, dry, and all vegetation die.

Everyone remembered to cap it.
Everyone. Always. Even while drinking
or filling pitchers, eyes stayed on
the lid, arms flexed, ready to put the cap back.

Ceremoniously.
Until the morning that Seta was sent
to fetch water for baking day.
She had to remove the heavy lid alone
because she had rushed off without waiting

for her sleepy sister. She had rushed off
taking two blue pitchers,
early in the morning, early in the day
when the sky was streaked with variegated light.

She met no one except handsome Movses who
was riding Keurkig, his ebony horse, to
his father's pastures. He too saw Seta
at the fountain and pulled in his rein
to turn his horse back to the spring.

Seta who watched him ride by, blushed
as she saw him turn. She looked away,
back at her pitcher as he rode back.
She filled both pitchers slowly, telling

herself to hurry home. Another Seta
answered saying, but isn't this what
you were hoping when you started out,
not waiting for dawdling Sophie?
Her heart began another rhythm and her feet
had trouble moving over the pebbles.
How absurd to be so agitated over someone
with whom she had not exchanged a word.
How strange to be in love when she was too young
to love. How odd

that such a pale sun could redden her cheeks
and the bridge of her nose.
Movses reached the fountain, paused
before dismounting. His eyes and smile
were bold but there was a small flame
in his cheek too. And his hand shook
with a sudden chill. But his voice
was firm. "I'm glad your pitcher is blue
because I am very thirsty and only a blue
pitcher would do." He dismounted
and continued, "Filled with cold Sevan
water by you."

She looked up and wondered at
the voice answering him boldly.
Wondered who could be speaking haughtily,
even coldly, when a shudder overtook
her heart?

Where did her calm come from? From where
the voice that spoke? "Ride on.
The water I am drawing is very warm."

"Ride on," the voice insisted. "It will not
quench the thirst of a bee." She remembered

the song of Mt. Mensour. She remembered.
So did he,

how the girls who drew water at Mt. Mensour.
laughed at the horsemen riding by. Movses laughed
remembering what she recalled. Both stood grinning
and staring, coils of folk poems linking them.

When they laughed,. his horse tossed its mane
and Seta laughed, "This water is dangerous,
it casts a terrible spell."

"Let it happen," he quoted the old poem
"exactly as you tell. Let it be as
if my mother never bore a son."
And he took the blue pitcher and reached
for her hand as he drank.

By the time she refilled the pitcher,
by the time he mounted his horse,
said farewell and rode up the hills,
by the time they had parted, she completely
forgot the wooden lid of the well.

The spring bubbled and rose. It rose and bubbled,
it covered the lid and turned it to gold.
As she rode homeward and Movses rode on,
it rose and surged, rose and flowed, turning
its path to silver. Although it was only
a trickle, it widened. It widened to
a narrow stream, then a river, until
everything was flooded. The village streets,
the gardens, the floors changed to pools.

With a great whinny the animals all bolted.
The villagers ran without saving a pin.

Someone shouted a curse, "A curse
on the forgetful one who left off the cap
of the spring. May he turn to stone."

Seta stumbled and fell then, and could run
no more. Her legs stopped their moving.
Water reached her, rushed about her,
became Lake Sevan, while she became a stone.

Movses rode down from the hill in time
to find a flood where his house had been.
Movses came back from the hills to find
a stone where his love was last seen,
a sea that heaved like her breathing.
Movses went to the edge of the lake
unfathomable as sleep,
new and mysterious with stars
that flecked its waves.

Lake Sevan was not always salty.
Movses's tears gave it that salt.
And the stone in the lake's center
was named for the bride Movses
never had: Brideshead Stone
for the sea he did not swim.

MAY

Even its name fills
with possibilities: "Yes,
you may." Month of blossoming,
month of true beginnings
and the soft perfume
of petals when it rains,
month of Maia, month of Mary
and month in which to praise
kept and unkempt gardens
and outdoor days.

DESIRE

The bee too
heavy by design
to levitate,
whirs and tries.
With furry lines
and power all wrong
it flies.

Is it because
bees don't know laws
of physics to
analyse
their flaws?
Flower to flower
they simply rise.

YARN

On Twelfth Night in the greenery outside
my window you hung a red yarn ball
in the pine branches eye level
to prolong the Christmastide.

Now it is March. A cardinal absorbed
in preening, lands in the tree
branches as if it seeking company
of its own chroma, making two red orbs.

He stares at me, staring back, then yawns.
Or perhaps a wind drowns his cry
leaving its unheard echo on the eye.
The bird nods to the yarn and he is gone

leaving your return and his song
hanging with the yarn all year long.

ABOUT THE AUTHOR

This is Diana Der-Hovanessian's 15th volume of poetry. She has won awards from the National Endowment of the Arts, Poetry Society of America, Columbia University Translation Center, Fulbright Commission for Exchange of Scholars, and Quarterly Review of Literature. She lectures on American poetry and the literature of human rights, and conducts poetry workshops at various universities.

PUBLICATIONS BY DIANA DER-HOVANESSIAN

How to Choose Your Past, Ararat Press, Saddle Brook, NJ
About Time, Ashod Press, New York
Inside Green Eyes, Black Eyes, translated into Armenian, Sovetpress, Yerevan,
　　Armenia
Songs of Bread, Songs of Salt, Ashod Press, New York
Selected Poems, Sheep Meadow Press, Riverdale, NY
Valley of Flowers, Armen Press, Yerevan, Armenia

TRANSLATIONS

Anthology of Armenian Poetry, Columbia University Press, New York (winner of
　　P.E.N./Translation Center and Kolligian Awards)
Land of Fire, Selected Poems of Eghishe Charents, Ardis Press, Ann Arbor,
　　MI (winner of Van de Bovenkamp, Armand Erpf Awards for excellence
　　in literary translation)
Sacred Wrath, Selected Poems of Vahan Tekeyan, Ashod Press, New York
The Arc, Selected Poems of Shen-Mah, St. Vartan Press, New York (The above
　　four edited with M. Margossian)
Come Sit Beside Me and Listen to Kouchag (Medieval Armenian poems) Ashod
　　Press, New York
Selected Poems of Gevorg Emin, International Poetry Forum Press, Pittsburgh, PA
　　(limited edition)
For You on New Year's Day, Selected Poems of Gevorg Emin, Ohio University
　　Press, Athens, OH
Coming to Terms, Selected Poems of Vahan Derjan, Ashod Press, New York
Across Bucharest After Rain, Maria Banus, Quarterly Review of Literature,
　　Princeton, NJ